Everything You Need to Know About

GETTING YOUR PERIOD

Getting your period is just one sign of the many changes during adolescence.

• THE NEED TO KNOW LIBRARY •

Everything You Need to Know About

GETTING YOUR PERIOD

Nancy Rue

THE ROSEN PUBLISHING GROUP, INC.
NEW YORK

Published in 1995 by The Rosen Publishing Group, Inc.
29 East 21st Street, New York, NY 10010

First Edition

Manufactured in the United States of America

Library of Congress Cataloging-in-Publication Data

Rue, Nancy N.
    Everything you need to know about getting your period / Nancy N.
Rue.
        p.   cm. — (The Need to know library)
    Includes bibliographical references and index.
    ISBN 0-8239-1870-X
    1. Menstruation—Juvenile literature. [1. Menstruation.]
I. Title. II. Series.
QP263.R84   1995
612.6′62—dc20   94-42067
                                                        CIP
                                                        AC

Contents

Introduction

Katie's 12—and she's facing a huge step in her life. She's about to start her first period.

Anyone will tell you that getting your period is a normal part of becoming a woman. But Katie is like many girls between the ages of 12 and 16. She has a lot of questions about getting her period, or **menstruation** as it's called. But she's too shy to ask them.

This book is for girls like Katie. Maybe you're one of them. You're waiting for the day to come, but you're not ready for it. And no one is telling you how to get ready.

Or maybe you've already started your period, but some things about it still have you puzzled. This book can help you, too.

Many changes go along with getting your period, and they happen fast. First you find, or will soon find, blood on your underwear or toilet paper. That can make you look twice.

Then you have to use protection for about a week so blood won't get on your clothes. You have to remember to change the pad or tampon. And you have to deal with the fear that blood will get on your jeans, your desk at school, everywhere.

And you're facing this whole thing happening over and over, once a month, until you're about fifty years old.

So go ahead and be nervous. But keep in mind that all of that change and responsibility is positive. It all means you are becoming a woman.

Getting your period may not be exactly fun, but it's part of being a woman. Because you have periods, you can have babies someday.

Talking to your friends may be helpful if you're worried about getting your period.

Chapter 1

Learning the System

Menstruation is part of your **reproductive system**, your baby-making equipment. Let's look at that system.

The **sex** organs or **genital organs** have to do with producing babies. The outside of the female organs is called the **vulva**.

If you look at your naked body in a mirror, you'll see an area between your legs where your hip bones form a kind of arch. That's the **pubic area**. The bone in the center is the pubic bone. And the hair that is starting to cover it is the pubic hair.

Outside Your Body

Mons. The mons is the pad of fatty tissue that covers the pubic area and pubic bone. Pubic hair is probably starting to grow in this area.

Outer Lips. Looking in the mirror, you can see that the mons divides into two folds of skin that

look a little like lips. The outer lips are called the
labia majora (that's Latin for "greater lips").

Inner Lips. If you separate the outer lips, you'll
see the inner lips. The scientific name for these is
the **labia minora** ("small lips").

Clitoris. This is the small organ where the
inner lips join at the top. The clitoris is sensitive to
the touch.

Urethra. The urethra is a tiny opening straight
down from the clitoris where urine is passed from
your bladder.

Vaginal Opening. Down from the urethra is the
opening that leads to your internal sex organs.

Hymen. This is a layer of skin that stretches
across your vaginal opening. Many girls have a
hymen (or "cherry"); some don't. If it's there, it
has an opening to let fluids like menstrual blood
flow out. The hymen can be broken by gymnastics,
or it can just dissolve, so not having one is not
"proof" that a girl has had sex.

Inside Your Body

The sex organs inside your body are called your
reproductive organs.

Vagina. This is the passageway leading to the
inside of your body. It's four or five inches long,
and it expands. When you consider that a baby
passes through there as it's born, you can see that
it expands a lot. Your menstrual blood passes out

through the vagina. This is also where the man's penis enters during sexual intercourse.

Cervix. The cervix is at the far end of the vagina. You can feel it with your middle finger. It's a bump, rather like a pencil eraser. It's only about one inch in diameter in an adult woman. The little hollow in the center of the cervix is the **os**, where the blood leaves your body during your period. It's also where the sperm passes in during sexual intercourse.

Uterus. Also called the **womb**, this is an organ about the size of your fist, shaped like a pear turned upside down. Its walls are made of strong, stretchy muscle. Its lining builds up each month to provide an unborn baby with nourishment. If no baby is conceived during the month, the body sheds that lining. That's called menstruation.

Fallopian Tubes. These two tubes extend from the top sides of the uterus. They're four inches long but only about as thick as a needle. On the outer end of each tube is a fringe called **fimbria**.

Ovaries. An almond-shaped ovary lies on either side of your uterus close to your fallopian tubes. When you were born, each of your ovaries contained about 400,000 eggs called **ova** (one is called an **ovum**). Your ovaries make the female hormones **estrogen** and **progesterone**.

Chapter 2

The Changes of Puberty

Katie's 12, and she's grossed out every time she looks in the mirror. Check out all those blackheads and pimples.

Justine is in the seventh grade. She's grown four inches this year, and all she sees are the tops of boys' heads. She feels like a giant.

Cianna wakes up one morning and suddenly—at least it seems so to her—she has breasts and hips and hair under her arms. At 15, she's been waiting for it to happen since she was 11. But now that it's here it's a little overwhelming.

What Katie and Justine and Cianna are experiencing are the changes that take place in the body when the reproductive system matures and the hormones start to function.

Hormones

Hormones are chemicals that are formed in

FEMALE REPRODUCTIVE ORGANS

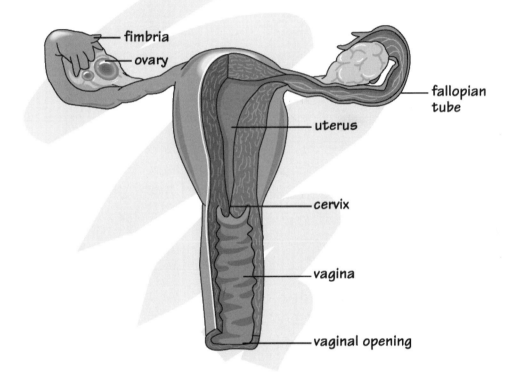

Your entire body goes through changes when you reach adolescence.

certain organs of your body. When a hormone is produced in one organ or gland, it goes to another part of your body to go to work.

You have hundreds of hormones that keep your body behaving normally, but two, **estrogen** and **progesterone**, are not produced until puberty. These two, somewhere between age 8 and age 18, tell your body to change.

Progesterone has more to do with menstruation itself. Estrogen causes:

- development of breasts
- widening of hips and buttocks
- growth of pubic and armpit hair
- production of more oil in skin and hair
- thickening of the hair on your legs
- increase in perspiration
- interest in romance and sexual feelings.

There are three often-asked questions that estrogen can answer for you.

(1) **Why is my face breaking out?** Hormones, estrogen mostly, cause the oil glands in your skin to produce more. The result is blackheads, whiteheads, cysts, and pimples.

(2) **Why am I growing so fast?** These hormones are working double time. Since age two, you've grown about two inches a year. When puberty starts, that rate can double to four inches a year. In middle school the boys, who have their growing spurt later, may only be up to your chin.

After your first period the growth rate slows to about an inch a year until you level off in your mid-teens.

(3) **Why am gaining weight?** Right when a slim figure would make life easier, you may start noticing fatty tissue in your breasts, hips, thighs, stomach, upper arms, and even your face. That's normal weight gain caused by those clever little hormones.

What Can I Do About Hormones?

Well, nothing. Although the changes they cause are confusing and sometimes embarrassing, usually, by about age 18, girls pretty much like what they see in the mirror.

"But what about now?" you wail.

Here are a few suggestions.

These zits! About 80 percent of all teenagers are affected by acne, which is the medical term for the skin disorder.

Acne is activated by the hormone **androgen**. Along with estrogen, androgen causes your oil glands to produce more of the fatty substance called **sebum**. If you have acne, instead of emptying out of the oil gland openings, the cells clump together and plug up the glands.

No one is sure why some teenagers get acne and some don't. Some doctors think it may have to do with heredity.

So what do you do about it?

- Remember that mild cases usually clear up by themselves with time.
- Keep your skin and hair clean, and keep your hair away from your face.
- If you wear makeup, choose the nonoily variety. Always remove it before you go to bed.
- Don't pick at or squeeze blackheads, whiteheads, or pimples.

If your acne really seems out of control, see a skin doctor (dermatologist).

Sweat! Cianna noticed that all her blouses were getting stained under the arms. She was also aware of a new odor.

Your changing hormones are also changing the makeup of your sweat. It now creates a sometimes unpleasant odor, especially in your armpits. Here are some tips to help you control the odor:

- Wash every day with soap.
- Shave under your arms regularly. The fuzz can hold the warmth and moisture that give bacteria the perfect place to grow.
- Use a plain deodorant, which protects against odor but doesn't control sweating.
  Avoid using antiperspirants, which work to stop sweating with either aluminum or zinc salts. If you sweat a lot, try wearing materials that "breathe," like cotton.

I feel fat! Justine doesn't care that it's "just

hormones" that have caused her to gain weight. She'd still like to feel comfortable in a bathing suit. Putting on some pounds is normal during this time, but unfortunately some girls start bad eating habits to try to control their weight that can be pretty hard to break later. A few suggestions for avoiding that trap:

- Remember that your basic body frame can't be changed. If you're tall, you're tall. If your hip bones are set wide apart, you have hips. If you wear size ten shoes, hey, that's the way it is.
- Remember that everybody can look good. The first step is to dump the idea that you need to look like Cindy Crawford. Go for your own best look.
- Eat a healthful diet. If you don't know how to do that, get a nutrition book, or ask your doctor.
- Get into the habit of exercising. Find something you like to do that burns calories and go for it. Go dancing, play basketball, grab some friends and go bike riding—it all works as long as you do it at least three times a week for 30 minutes.
- Experiment with styles that flatter your figure. Just because your friend wears the spandex skirt and the midriff blouse doesn't mean you have to. And you can still look terrific!

Chapter 3

How Does Your Period Work?

We have already talked about how estrogen causes changes in your body. Estrogen also sets off another process that causes you to have your period.

Take another look at the diagram of your reproductive organs on page 13. Zero in on your ovaries first and then follow the steps below.

Step one. Sometime during puberty, a ripened egg will burst from one of your ovaries. That is **ovulation**. It will happen every month.

Step two. The fringe around the fallopian tube, the fimbria, reaches out to move the egg toward the fallopian tube. There tiny hairs push the egg along down into the uterus so it will be in place to meet a sperm.

Step three. If you were to have sexual intercourse during that time, the sperm could meet the egg and one of the sperm could break through the egg's outer shell. The egg would be fertilized. You'd be pregnant.

Step four. If it is not fertilized, the egg moves down the fallopian tube to the uterus. By this time, the estrogen has caused your uterus to build a lining of tissue and blood. When you don't become pregnant, that lining is discharged through the cervix and the vagina. That's your period.

It sounds simple, but you probably have some questions. These are a few that many girls ask.

Exactly what is the discharge? Part of it is blood. The rest is uterine lining and mucus from your cervix and vagina.

Does it come out all at once? Usually menstrual blood dribbles out slowly over three to five days. It may last from two days to eight.

For most girls the flow is heaviest the first day or two, then tapers off. The color will probably be brownish-red at the start, go to dark red in the middle, and back to brownish-red at the end. You might pass dark red clumps called clots. They are parts of the uterine lining.

Somebody told me you could bleed at other times, too. It isn't unusual to find a few blood spots in the middle of your cycle, at the time of ovulation. If you spot more than that, you should probably see a doctor.

What is the "menstrual cycle"? The time between the start of your period until the start of your your next one is an average of 28 days. The

You can keep track of your menstrual cycle on a calendar.

interval can be as short as 21 days or as long as 35. The cycle has four phases.

Phase one lasts three to seven days. During that time blood and the uterine lining are being discharged from your body. Estrogen and progesterone are at their lowest levels. That can make you feel tired and grumpy.

Phase two is about two to four days after your period stops. Your pituitary gland has sent a message to your ovaries to resume producing estrogen. Another egg starts to ripen. Estrogen is pumping once more, so you feel pretty good.

Phase three is right in the middle of your

cycle, about 8 to 14 days after your period started.

Estrogen reaches its highest level around day 14. The egg breaks out from the ovary. Progesterone is at its highest level, because it is preparing the uterine lining. Some girls feel mild discomfort the day they ovulate.

Phase four starts about day 15. If the egg hasn't been fertilized, production of estrogen and progesterone lessens. The uterine lining gets ready to leave the body. You may feel bloated and fat and cranky and moody. We're talking about the famous PMS here, which we'll discuss later.

How will I know when my period will start? You can have your first period anywhere from age 9 to age 18. Usually a girl's first period occurs about two years after her breasts develop.

You may also notice an occasional white discharge from your vagina several months before you actually get your period. Then it may turn brown for a while, and finally be red menstrual blood.

Some girls notice their stomachs looking and feeling bloated. Others have warning cramps, or their back hurts or their breasts are tender. The following are the most common symptoms: queasy stomach or cramps; swollen, tender breasts; a major outbreak of pimples; emotional feelings; hair oilier than usual; more perspiration than usual; a little weight gain; tense and irritable feelings; unusual hunger and thirst; fatigue or an "I don't care" attitude; lower back ache; and headache.

Chapter 4

Dealing with It!

For most girls, the problem with having your period is not so much knowing what's happening to your body as what to do when it does happen. How do you use a pad? What about tampons? What about toxic shock syndrome?

Following are questions girls usually have.

"What do I do if I'm at school and my period starts for the first time?"

First off, you need "feminine protection." Most girls start with pads. They're easy to use and they keep things pretty simple those first few months.

A pad is merely several layers of soft cotton made to absorb liquid. It has an adhesive strip on one side. Peel the strip off and place that side against the crotch of your panties.

Pads come in different shapes and sizes. Many women prefer a thicker pad the first few days, when the flow is heavier. Then you can switch to

It is a good idea to be prepared with pads or tampons in case your period starts unexpectedly.

the thin ones when your period slows down.

Variations in styles may seem confusing at first. Ask your friends what they use and like.

If you don't have an emergency supply of pads, borrow a pad from a friend or see if there is a vending machine for them in the girls' restroom. If all else fails, go to the school nurse.

"What do I do if I'm someplace where there just aren't any pads?"

I was at the circus with my grandfather when I got my first period at age 12. I wish someone had given me this piece of advice. If no pads are available, fold up some toilet paper, paper towels, or tissue and place it in the crotch of your underwear until you can get a pad. The main thing is not to be embarrassed to ask someone for help. Ask even that nice woman who is combing her hair next to you if she has a spare one in her purse. We've all been there, and we like to help.

"How often do I have to change my pad?"

Change your pad according to your own flow. The general rule is to change every two or three hours during the first half of your period and every four or five hours the second half. Pads have a plastic lining between layers of soft cotton to keep blood from leaking through. But if you wear a pad too long, blood can leak out the sides, and an odor develops when menstrual blood contacts the air.

"What do I do if I bleed through my clothes?"

Many products are available to help you cope with the body changes that come with puberty.

Your best bet is prevention. When you know it's time for your period, wear a pad even before you start bleeding.

But sometimes your period can sneak up on you, and there you are with a stain on the back of your skirt. It's no big deal:

- Change into the extra jeans you've learned to keep in your locker.
- Call home and ask your parent to bring you a change of clothes.
- Zip out of your skirt, wash it with soap and cold water in the restroom sink, and dry it with the hand dryer.
- Go to the school nurse. In some schools, the nurse keeps extra clothes on hand or will let you dash home with an off-campus pass.

Once again, the trick is not to think your life is over or you can never show your face again. Linda started her period in white jeans, and her friend Tim said, "Hey, Linda, did you sit in chocolate?" Most people, even guys, figure it's part of growing up. If they don't—that's their problem!

If you do bleed onto your clothes, soak them in cold water and detergent before you put them in the washer. Blood stains are tough to get out.

"Mom is always lecturing me about not flushing pads down the toilet. How *am* I supposed to get rid of them?"

When you change your pad, roll it into a ball,

wrap toilet or tissue paper around it, and pop it into the trash can. Public restrooms usually have a metal container in every stall for that purpose.

"What is it that I smell when I change my pad? Can other people smell it when they're around me?"

That "fishy" odor is really two things. One, it's the germs in your menstrual blood mixing with the air. And two, it's caused by estrogen producing mucus in your body so the blood can flow. If you take care of yourself this way, no one else will be able to smell it:

• Change your pad often.
• Take a bath or shower every day.
• Wear clean underwear every day—and change it whenever blood gets on it.

Personal cleanliness is all you need. Take care of yourself, and you won't have to give odor a second thought.

"What about tampons?"

A tampon is a narrow tube of absorbent cotton. It's designed to be inserted right into the vagina. Your vagina is flexible so it molds itself around the tampon. The tampon is like a sponge; it becomes larger as it takes in fluid.

A tampon has many advantages over a pad:

• If you have it in right, you can't feel a thing.
• It's small enough to carry in your purse.

If you follow the rules for basic personal cleanliness, you can feel confident that any unpleasant odors are under control.

- There's less chance of odor than with a pad.
- You can't see it under a swimsuit.
- You can go swimming wearing a tampon.

There are several different types of tampons.

One type has a cardboard applicator. It has two tubes: One lets you insert the tampon smoothly; the other one pushes the tampon into place.

The type with the plastic applicator works almost the same way as the cardboard. Some girls like it better because it's smoother.

The type with no applicator is very small. It is often preferred by beginners with tampons.

Each type of tampon comes in sizes: junior, slender, regular, super, and extra-superabsorbent.

"I really want to try tampons, but how do you put it in?"

There is no mystery about putting in a tampon. Almost everyone is a little clumsy at first. Try these simple steps:

1. First of all, relax. Anxiety makes it harder to insert a tampon, because when you're nervous your vaginal muscles tighten. Take some good deep breaths. Sometimes it takes a couple of trys.

2. Know your own body. Really look at the diagrams and pictures in this book. Or look at your genitals with a mirror.

3. Start with the slender or junior size.

4. Find a comfortable position. Some girls stand with their knees slightly bent. Others put one foot up on the toilet seat. Still others sit on the toilet itself, although most beginners say it's harder when you're sitting down. One "tampon expert" suggests lying down the first time so you can really relax.

5. Take the wrapper off and hold the tampon in the hand you write with. If you're lying down, raise your knees and spread your legs slightly. Using your other hand, gently open the folds of skin around your vaginal opening. Place the tip of the tampon at your vaginal opening and push it inside just a little, maybe 1/4 to 1/2 inch. Then, if you're using a cardboard or plastic applicator, just push the smaller tube into the larger one. Now pull both tubes away. If instead you're using a tampon that has no

applicator, make sure you've loosened the string, and push the tampon in as far as you can.

6. Cardboard applicators can be flushed down the toilet, but probably shouldn't. To be on the safe side, toss them in the trash can. Plastic applicators should always be put in the wastebasket.

You know you have your tampon in right when:

- you can't feel it when you stand, sit, jump, squat, or lie down
- the string is hanging free, outside your vaginal opening
- you can see only the string and no other part of the tampon.

Taking a tampon out is really the easy part. Just pull gently on the string and it will slide right out. Be prepared for it to be larger now, because it has absorbed fluid. Even though tampons are made to be flushable, it's easier on the plumbing if you wrap them up and put them in the trash.

"I tried a tampon once but I couldn't get it in. What if it just doesn't work?"

First of all, just about everyone who's tried tampons has asked the same question. If you're having tampon troubles, try these tricks:

- Maybe your aim is bad. I was 21 years old before I figured out how to use a tampon

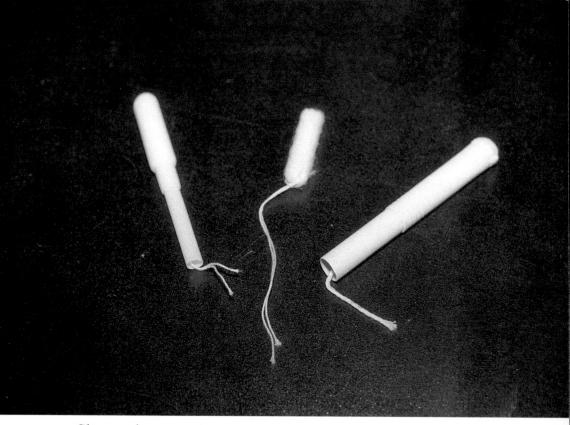

Choose the type of tampon that is most comfortable for you to use.

successfully. All through high school and college, every month I'd break out the box and the instructions. I had just about given up when one day I saw a side view of the female body in a diagram. Something caught my eye: The vagina doesn't go straight up. It kind of angles toward the small of your back. The next time I tried a tampon, I aimed it toward my lower back at a slant—and it went right in!

- Maybe your vagina is dry. Try putting some saliva or a lubricant like K-Y jelly on the tip of the tampon. Just don't use anything with perfume in it. That can irritate your vagina.
- Maybe you're pushing the tampon against the

skin. With your fingers, separate the folds of
skin and then try it.

- Maybe you're using the wrong size or type for
  you. If it seems too big, try junior or slender. Or
  try the no-applicator variety. If it won't slide, go
  for one with a plastic applicator. Ask your
  friends what works for them.
- Maybe you need a different position. There is
  no right or wrong way. Experiment until you
  find the right way for you.
- Maybe your body isn't ready. If you have tried
  all of the above, wait a few months and then try
  again. Your vaginal opening is narrow when
  you're young, but it naturally grows as you get
  older. It may be a few more months, or even a
  year or two before your body is ready for
  tampons. It's important to work with your body,
  not against it.
- Maybe you aren't ready. If you've just started
  having your period, you may still be struggling
  with the whole idea of it. Shelly, who is 15, has
  had her period for three years and just started
  using tampons. She suggests finding the most
  comfortable pad you can for a while. Get used to
  the idea of having your period. Then experiment
  with tampons if you want. There's no rush!
- If it really feels that something is blocking the
  way, talk to your mom or the school nurse or
  someone else you trust. You may need to have a
  doctor check it out. Whether you use tampons

There are several brands of tampons to choose from.

or not, anything that concerns you about your own body should be looked at.

"I tried a tampon and I found it painful! Did I do something wrong?"

The whole purpose of tampons is to provide a

comfortable way to get through your period. If it's uncomfortable, something's wrong. But don't despair. It can be fixed.

Usually if a tampon hurts or bothers you, it's because it isn't pushed in far enough. Just relax and push it in farther. If that doesn't work, pull it out and start over with a fresh one.

Shelly also suggests changing to a tampon that expands out instead of up. If you use one that gets longer as it fills up, it may have no place left to go. It will start being uncomfortable.

"Once I have the tampon in, can it get lost inside me?"

Not a chance! The only opening from your vagina to the rest of your body is the os, the tiny depression in the center of your cervix. This is the opening through which the menstrual blood leaves the uterus. A tampon absolutely cannot go through it. There's no other way it could get to any other part of your body.

"Will it fall out? That would be so embarrassing in gym class!"

It won't fall out if you have it in right. You'll know if it isn't in right because you'll be able to feel it. If you can't feel it, it's in there until you take it out by pulling the string. Your vagina is very flexible. It snuggles in around the tampon to hold it in place. There is also a ring-shaped muscle inside your vagina called the sphincter. Once the tampon is pushed past that, it also works to hold it in place. That's why it's important to push the tampon in far enough.

"I've heard tampons can make you sick. It that true?"

Vanessa was talking about **toxic shock syndrome**, or TSS. This is an extremely rare illness that has been connected with the use of super-absorbent tampons. Tampons are not the cause of toxic shock syndrome. It has been known to occur in women who don't use tampons, and even in children and men. Only about 17 out of every 100,000 menstruating women develop TSS each year.

TSS is a disease caused by bacteria. Bacteria live in your vagina all the time, and normally they are harmless. However, if a highly absorbent tampon is left in too long, those same bacteria can become dangerous.

To lower the risk of TSS, use the least absorbent tampons you can. Change them every two or three hours for the first few days of your period, then every four or five hours when the flow slows down. If you wear a tampon to bed, be sure you don't keep it in longer than eight hours.

Store tampons in a clean, dry place. Keep purse tampons in a little case so you aren't dumping your gum, wallet, and cash on top of them and tearing the paper so germs can get in. And always wash your hands with soap and water before inserting or removing a tampon.

If you have any of the symptoms of toxic shock syndrome during your period, remove your tampon right away and see your doctor. The symptoms include:

- fever
- aching muscles
- sore throat
- nausea
- vomiting
- headache
- big-time diarrhea
- sunburn-like rash
- peeling skin from hands and feet

If you use tampons the right way, you don't have to be worried about TSS. The brochure in the tampon box mentions it so the manufacturer cannot be accused of not telling you about some risk—however remote.

Chapter 5

Old Wives' Tales— and the Right Stuff

*T*here was a slumber party going on at *Heather's. She and Gina and Erica and Amy and Kelly had eaten one large pizza with extra pepperoni and had started on the second, when Gina came out of the bathroom and said, "I've got the curse. Anybody got a pad?"*

While Heather got up to get her one, Amy groaned to herself. She knew that the conversation was now going to turn to "getting your period." It always did after they had said everything about the other usual subjects—boys, clothes, teachers, and parents.

Why did they always end up talking about this? Amy wondered. She hated it. For one thing, all of them had already started their periods and she hadn't, even though she was almost 14. But worse than that, they always said stuff that, frankly, Amy wasn't sure was true. It didn't match what

You only lose about one quarter of a cup of blood during your entire period.

she'd read in that little book her mom had given her. But then, it was published in 1968 . . .

"Why don't you use tampons when you get your friend?" Erica said when Heather and Gina came back.

Gina's eyes grew wide. "Because," she said. "I'm a virgin."

"I don't know about that," Heather said. "I don't use them because my mom says they make you have worse cramps."

Kelly rolled her eyes. "It doesn't matter what I use. I still get cramps, and I get so tired I can hardly move. That's from the loss of blood."

"Really?" Gina said, her eyes getting even wider.

"How much blood do we lose, do you think?"

"A cup," Erica said. "Maybe more."

Kelly held up the mug she was drinking a Coke from and stared at it. "You mean, like this much?" she said.

Erica nodded, then said, "You know what I really hate about being on the rag?"

"What?" said Heather as she helped herself to another slice of pizza.

"Two things, really," Erica said. "Going to the dentist is one."

Heather stopped eating in mid-bite. "Going to the dentist? What does that have to do with it?"

Erica looked at her as if she were stupid. "Because, silly. The dentist can tell if you're on your period. Your gums look different or your breath smells a certain way or something."

Gina covered her mouth with her hand. "I'm so embarrassed! That's gross!"

"What's the other thing you hate, Erica?" Kelly said.

"Douching afterward."

They all stared at her.

"What's douching?" Heather said finally.

"Don't you guys do it?" Erica said.

"How do I know if I do it if I don't know what it is?" Kelly said.

Erica looked over her shoulder and lowered her voice. Everyone leaned in, including Amy. "I'm not going to go into the details," Erica whispered. "But it's a way of cleaning out—things—after

*your period. You know, to get all the smell and the
germs and stuff out. My mom says menstrual
blood is poison, so you really have to clean
yourself out when your period is over."*

Gina gasped. "I never do that!"

*"Well," Kelly said dryly, "you aren't dead yet, so
I guess you haven't been poisoned."*

*Erica glared at her and snatched up a piece of
pizza.*

*Heather cleared her throat. "Well, what I hate
is that you can't do anything. I mean, you can't
wash your hair. You can't do P.E. class. You can't
play sports. You can't even go swimming."*

*"I know," Kelly agreed. "You might as well just
stay in bed for the whole week."*

*There was a silence as everyone put down their
pizza slices and looked depressed.*

*"You want to watch a movie?" Heather said
finally.*

*The talk turned then to which video to watch,
but Amy didn't join in. She sat on the edge of
Heather's bed and tried to sort it out. Was all of
that stuff true? If it was, she definitely wished she
was a boy.*

Actually, Amy doesn't have to wish she weren't a
girl. Just about everything Erica, Heather, Gina,
and Kelly said about having their periods was
absolutely, completely, totally untrue.

They weren't lying. They were just repeating
things they'd heard. But some of the myths they

Sanitary pads are designed not to show through clothing.

were sharing with each other can keep a girl from enjoying life while she's having her period. Others can actually be hurtful. Let's look at those old wives' tales about menstruation and get some straight facts.

Myth #1. You can't use tampons if you're a virgin. If you do, you aren't a virgin anymore.

A virgin is a person who has never had sexual intercourse. Since that has nothing to do with tampons, that explodes that myth!

41

The confusion arises because at one time people thought the breaking of the hymen meant you weren't a virgin. Some girls are born without one. That doesn't mean they were never virgins! The hymen has an opening to allow fluid such as menstrual blood to pass out of the body. So it's perfectly fine to use a tampon.

Myth #2. Tampons give you bad cramps.

We are not exactly sure what causes cramps, but we know it has nothing to do with tampons. There is no connection between the use of tampons and the pain of menstrual cramps.

Myth #3. You lose about a cup of blood when you have your period.

The average female loses between one and six tablespoons of blood during her period. As you already know, that's mixed with other substances to make up the menstrual flow. That isn't very much at all, especially over the course of five to seven days. It isn't enough to make you weak.

Myth #4. The dentist can tell if you're on your period.

Only if you tell him or her!

I can't find any scientific basis for that statement. Besides, what difference would it make if the dentist could tell? Having your period isn't a reason to be embarrassed with a health care professional. Even if you're a private person, remember that it's a normal part of being a female.

Myth #5. You have to douche after your

period because menstrual blood is poison.

First of all, menstrual blood isn't "poison" any more than the saliva in your mouth or the sweat in your armpits is. It's a fluid that your own body makes, so it isn't poisonous to you.

Now, let's talk about douching. You've probably seen ads for vaginal douches or even noticed them in the drugstore. Douches are liquids designed to clean the vagina. But the vagina is self-cleaning. It's like your eyes. Unless you have something stuck in your eye that needs to be flushed out, you don't wash out your eyes on a regular basis. You don't need to do that for your vagina either. The only time you should douche is if your doctor or health practitioner says you should.

Myth #6. You can't wash your hair during your period.

There is no better time to wash your hair than during your period, because your body tends to produce more oil then. Go ahead and wash it. Look your best, because that will make you feel better, too. There is no medical evidence that washing your hair during your period is harmful to you in any way.

Myth #7. You can't be physically active during your period.

The amount of physical activity you do when you're having your period doesn't affect your period in any way. What you do during that one week every month should be determined by how you feel. If you feel like going skiing, playing volleyball, or dancing, go for it. If you have such bad cramps you can't even walk across the floor, don't try it. It's really a matter of common sense.

Some physical activity is actually good for you when you're having your period. You'll be amazed at how fast it can make mild cramps go away. And it's a known fact that exercise causes the creation of **endorphins**, which are "feel good" chemicals in your brain. By exercising you physically lift your spirits so that having your period just isn't so bad.

Myth #8. You can't go swimming during your period.

Swimming doesn't do anything to harm you when you're menstruating. It's just kind of a mess if you aren't using a tampon. With a tampon, no one will know you're having your period as long as you tuck the string into your suit.

Personally, I think it's the names we give to the menstrual periods that give rise to many mysterious and scary myths. Think about the ones the girls at the slumber party used:

"The curse"

"My friend" (said with sarcasm)

"That time of the month"

"Being on the rag"

No wonder we come up with all these horror stories. It's your menstrual period—a very natural thing. If you don't call it hate names, you probably won't hate it.

Chapter 6

What About the Pain?

*T*he alarm buzzed on the bedside table. 6:00 *a.m. Suzanne reached a hand out from under the covers to turn it off. As she came awake, she groaned.*

"Oh, no," she moaned to no one in particular. "Cramps again."

It was day number one of Suzanne's period. It was no surprise to her that she felt—well— miserable.

There were the cramps, of course, that made her feel as if her uterus was being tied into knots. And then there was the bloating. Her stomach looked like she'd swallowed a balloon—at least to her. Any minute now the headache would start, she thought as she dragged herself out of bed and went to the bathroom mirror. Big mistake. One look told her she was having the worst outbreak of pimples since—since her last period.

"I hate my period," she told the mirror. "I'm going back to bed until it's over."

Fortunately you don't have to crawl under the covers for five days out of every month to deal with the aches and pains and other problems that can come with your menstrual period. What you can do are two things:

- Understand what's going on with your body.
- Know the simple ways to get more comfortable.

Cramps

The most common negative thing attached to having your period is cramps. Menstrual cramps can give you anything from mild discomfort to severe pain, and they may differ from one time of your life to another. Some women say they always had cramps until after they had children. Others don't develop them until they're in their forties heading toward menopause (when menstruation stops completely).

Doctors are not sure why cramps often go with menstruation. There are a number of theories:

- Excess blood in the pelvic area.
- A tipped uterus, which would explain why some girls have them and some don't.
- Poor diet.

Some women feel symptons of PMS before and during their period.

- Contractions of the uterus to expel all the fluid.
- Hormones out of balance.

We do know that your body has high levels of chemicals called prostaglandins. These seem to cause the muscles of the uterus to cramp.

What do you do about cramps? The following are tried and true remedies:

- Exercise three times a week, even when you're not having your period, to build up your back and abdominal muscles.
- Stay on a good, nutritious diet—all the time!
- Once cramps hit, soothe them with heat— heating pad, hot water bottle, hot bath.

47

- Try over-the-counter pain relievers. Some are designed for menstrual cramps. Other remedies that contain aspirin, acetaminophen, or ibuprofen work for a lot of women.
- If your cramps are fairly mild, do a little mild exercise to match.
- If, on the other hand, your cramps are severe enough to keep you in bed or completely out of things, call your doctor. Prescription medications can reduce prostaglandins.

Bloat

Bloating, especially right before your period, is one of the most frustrating parts of the whole thing. Usually it happens because your body is retaining water. You may notice it in your stomach, breasts, hands, thighs, and even your face. What to do about it?

- Get plenty of vitamin B.
- Exercise regularly.
- Cut down on your salt intake, especially from two weeks before your period until it actually starts.
- It sounds strange—but drink a lot of water. Water helps flush out the stuff your body is holding onto.
- If bloating is a major problem, see your doctor. He may be able to prescribe a diuretic to get rid of excess fluid as you urinate.

Retaining water can also make your breasts tender just before or during your period. If so, try wearing a bra that holds them firmly.

Zits

It's thought that the outbreak of pimples just before or during your period is due to the increase in androgens (male hormones). Androgens make the oil glands produce more oil, which in turn gives rise to pimples. There isn't much you can do to prevent it, but you can do things that make it easier to live with.

- Apply a drying lotion that contains sulfur, salicylic acid, or benzol peroxide. Follow the directions on the package very carefully.
- Once you've done that and it has dried, cover the pimple with a foundation a shade lighter than your skin color.
- Cream cover-ups designed to hide blemishes are available. Follow one of those with a water-based foundation and dust on some powder.
- Don't use oil-based cosmetics. What you don't need is more oil!

PMS

PMS (premenstrual syndrome) is not a joke. It is a very real physical problem that happens to some women seven to ten days before their periods. It happens when the level of estrogen, that "feel good" hormone, drops. When it drops, so does your good mood!

The drop in estrogen can also contribute to hunger, thirst, crying jags, fatigue, depression, and mood swings.

Try some of these solutions, which have worked for a lot of other girls:

- Exercise.
- Snack on carbohydrates just before your period and for the first few days. Oatmeal cookies, saltines, and popcorn work really well.
- Get at least eight hours of sleep a night.
- Eat regular meals with not too much sugar or caffeine. Go big on vitamin B—green veggies, whole grains, and nuts.
- Accept PMS as part of the big picture. Give yourself a break. Do things you really like to do. Pamper yourself.

Muscle Aches

Heidi complains that when she gets her period she feels as if she's been working out 24 hours a day. Every muscle seems to ache, and she's so tired she can barely drag around.

While your estrogen level is going down, your level of progesterone, the other hormone, is going up. That can make you feel very tired. It also boosts the production of lactic acid, the stuff that makes your muscles feel sore when you exercise.

If you're feeling achy, try getting plenty of sleep and exercising. Keep the exercise sensible, though. Really strenuous physical training can cause irregular or even missed periods.

Irregular Periods

Ginnie had her first period when she was 12. Exactly a month later she had her second. Then her body seemed to "turn off," and she didn't have another period for six months. Of course, it came when she was at camp, totally unprepared. "I'd forgotten I was even supposed to have them!" she said. "I was borrowing pads from everyone. I totally ran out of underwear. It was the worst week I ever spent!"

What happened to Ginnie isn't uncommon. A lot of it is just being young. Menstruating is a new process. It could take a while to get regular. Just always be prepared—pads and extra clothes in your locker, your suitcase, your purse, your backpack.

Sometimes irregular periods are caused by other things. If any of these apply to you, try correcting the problem.

A heating pad can help relieve cramps.

- Poor eating habits, such as dieting, bingeing and purging, unhealthful foods, or not eating enough.
- Change of environment—moving to a new town or visiting a place with a very different altitude.
- Big weight gain or loss.
- Emotional upset or excitement.
- Physical problems such as illness or injury.
- Alcohol or drug abuse.

After you deal with your period for a few months, you'll find ways to take care of yourself, and none of the things that go along with it will seem so bad. But if anything that happens during your period seriously limits your ability to enjoy your life or to function the way you usually do, see your doctor.

Chapter 7

If Your Period Takes You to the Doctor

*E*rica had been having periods like clockwork for two years. Then suddenly, they became irregular. They would be 40 days apart one month, and then only 20 the next. Not only was it a bother, but she and her mom were becoming concerned. So they made an appointment with the doctor.

In the week between the phone call and the appointment, Erica broke out in a cold sweat every time she thought about it! This, she decided, was going to be so embarrassing. In fact, she knew she was going to be bright red during the entire physical, or even throw up or start crying.

And besides, what if something really weird were wrong with her? What if she had cancer? What if she found out she could never have children? By the time she walked into the examining room, she was a basket case.

Although I can think of more fun things to do than visit a gynecologist (the official name for a doctor who treats women), a pelvic exam (the name for the examination of the female sex organs) doesn't have to be a terrifying experience. Like every other part of becoming a woman, dealing with your doctor easily just means being prepared.

When You Need to See Your Doctor

- You're completely soaking a pad or tampon every hour for a day or two during your period.
- Your period lasts for more than a week with no signs of stopping.
- Your cycles are less than 28 days apart or more than 35 days apart.
- You are spotting blood at times other than when you ovulate for more than three cycles. (Remember that you ovulate about 14 days from the first day of your period.)
- You have severe menstrual cramps lasting more than three days a month.
- You have severe cramps when you're not having your period.
- You've had regular cycles for a year or more and then they become irregular.
- You're having burning vaginal discharges or severe vaginal itching.

- You're eighteen and have never had a pelvic exam before.

When You Don't Need to See Your Doctor

- If you've been having your period for only a year or less and your cycle is irregular. That's common and no cause for concern.
- Your periods are irregular or you're having more uncomfortable symptoms than usual (like cramps or pimples) *and* one or more of the following is happening at the same time: high excitement, heavy stress, poor diet, illness, change of environment, or sudden weight change.

What Is a Pelvic Exam?

Basically, it's the examination of the female reproductive organs to be sure they're healthy. A regular doctor or a health practitioner can do a pelvic exam. A gynecologist specializes in female sex organs.

Things to Do Before the Exam

- Ask your mother or a friend to go with you the first time if you're feeling anxious. It's relaxing to have somebody to chat with in the waiting room.

- Schedule your appointment for a time when you're not having your period. Since the doctor will examine you internally, menstruation makes that difficult.
- Take a shower before you go.
- Know this information, since it will probably appear on a form you will fill out in the office:
  - your health history (if you've ever had surgery or serious illnesses)
  - your family's health history (if anyone in your family has diabetes, cancer, etc.)
  - the first day of your last period
  - exactly what problem has brought you in.

What Will Happen Before the Exam

Usually, a nurse will take your height and weight, check your heart, and take your blood pressure. The nurse may also ask you about any problems you're having with your period. This would be a good time to say that this is your first exam. You will probably be asked to go to the restroom and leave a small urine sample in a container. Whether you do that or not, be sure to go to the bathroom before the exam so you'll be more comfortable.

What Happens During the Exam

The nurse will take you to an examining room
and ask you to undress completely. You'll be given
a gown or a sheet to cover yourself with, and you'll
be allowed to undress in private. Most health
professionals are very sensitive about the dignity
of their patients.

Once you've done that, you'll sit on the edge
of the examining table, which is covered with a
paper lining. When the doctor comes in, he or
she will chat with you for a minute about what's
bothering you, even though you've already written
it on the form and discussed it with the nurse.
Part of that is because the doctor can gain a lot of
information just by the way you describe your
symptoms.

A good thing to know is that a male
gynecologist must have a female nurse present
during the exam. You have the right to request
that one be present if one is not.

The doctor will examine your breasts for any
abnormal lumps. He or she will gently press on
your breasts and nipples and under your arms for
any signs of disease. Some doctors talk with you
while they're doing it to put you at ease. Most
don't even look during the exam. They can find
out what they need to know just by touch.

Then you will be asked to lie down and place
your feet in the metal stirrups at the end of the
examining table. You'll have to scoot down until

your bottom is right at the end of the table. You'll feel like you're going to fall off. You'll also feel awkward the first time, and that's to be expected. But with a sheet covering you and some light chatter going on, it's less uncomfortable than you'd think.

In this position, the doctor will be able to look inside you and check out many internal organs. He or she will use an instrument called a speculum to hold open the vaginal walls so he or she can see into the vaginal and cervical areas. This is completely painless, and it isn't even uncomfortable if you relax. Try some deep breaths and remember that it doesn't take long.

The doctor may then do a Pap test or Pap smear to check for cancer of the cervix. This disease is rare in young women, but a doctor just likes to be sure. A long cotton swab is inserted into your vagina, and cells from your cervix are gently scraped off. The doctor pulls out the swab and puts the cells on a slide, which is then sent to a laboratory. During a Pap test you may feel a dull sensation, but it usually isn't even as painful as having your finger pricked for blood. You may bleed just a little.

The doctor will then remove the speculum. He or she will next check to see that your uterus, cervix, fallopian tubes, and ovaries are okay. Wearing rubber gloves with a little gel on the fingertips, the doctor will put one or two fingers inside your vagina and place the other hand on your abdomen, pressing to feel the internal organs. He or she may also put one or two fingers inside your anus, again to confirm that everything is healthy.

And that's it! You're done! After the first exam especially, the doctor will probably give you a chance to talk more about anything that's bothering you or that you don't understand. This is the time to ask questions. If the doctor has found any problems or has advice for you, you'll get it now.

And Then I Never Have to Go Back Again, Right?

Well—wrong. Once you're 18, you really should have a pelvic exam every year. You can stay ahead of any problems by having a yearly Pap smear. A doctor can also detect other difficulties even before they start giving you symptoms.

If you felt uncomfortable or uneasy with the doctor you've visited, try another physician next time. Ask your friends whom they see. It's important to have a good relationship with your gynecologist. The two of you are a team in taking care of your body.

Glossary—*Explaining New Words*

androgen   Male hormone that causes the breakout of pimples in acne.

cervix   Opening in the lower part of the uterus.

clitoris   Small organ at the top of the labia minor; sensitive to the touch, it is thought to be one center of sexual pleasure in a female.

endorphins   "Feel good" chemicals in the brain.

estrogen   Hormone that helps direct body changes at puberty and reproduction.

hymen   Layer of skin that stretches across the vaginal opening in some girls at birth.

menstrual cramps   Discomfort or pain during the menstrual period.

ovaries   Two small organs on either side of the uterus where eggs are stored.

Pap test (or Pap smear)   Test for cancer in which cells from the cervix are examined.

progesterone   Hormone involved in the menstrual process.

prostaglandins   Chemicals whose level rises during menstruation.

tampon   Narrow tube of absorbent cotton to catch menstrual flow.

vulva   The female genitals (or external sex organs).

Where to Get Help

American College of Obstetricians and
    Gynecologists
409 12th Street SW
Washington, DC 20024
(202) 638-5577

National Women's Health Network
1325 G Street NW
Washington, DC 20005
(202) 347-1140

Planned Parenthood Federation of America,
    Educational Resources
810 Seventh Avenue
New York, NY 10019
(212) 541-7800

PMS Access
P.O. Box 9326
Madison, WI 53715
(800) 222-4767

For Further Reading

Mahoney, Ellen Voelckers. *Now You've Got Your Period*. New York: Rosen Publishing Group, Inc., 1993.

Madaras, Lynda. *The What's Happening to My Body? Book for Girls*. New York: Newmarket Press, 1987.

Marzollo, Jean. *Getting Your Period. A Book About Menstruation*. New York: Dial Books, 1989.

Index

About the Author
Nancy Rue received her B.A. in English from Stetson
University, DeLand, Florida, and her M.A. in education
from the College of William and Mary, Williamsburg,
Virginia. She worked for six years as a high school teacher,
then turned to free-lance writing. She is the author of six
books and more than fifty short stories, articles, and plays.
Ms. Rue lives with her husband and daughter in Reno,
Nevada.

Photo Credits
Cover by Lauren Piperno; pp. 2, 20, 23, 25, 34 by Marcus
Shaffer; pp. 8, 28, 32, 39, 42, 48, 53 by Kim Sonsky, p. 28 by
Michael Brandt

DATE DUE

AUG 1 5 1997		
FEB 1 9 1998	NOV 1 4 2000	
APR 2 4 1998		
	SEP 0 4 2001	
JUN 2 0 1998	OCT 1 1 2001	
	OCT 2 4 2002	
AUG 0 3 1998		
NOV 0 6 1998	AUG 2 8 2003	
FEB 1 6 1999	DEC 1 7 2003	
APR 1 0 1999	MAY 0 2 2005	
MAY 2 7 1999		
JUL 2 7 1999		
SEP 1 4 1999		
FEB 0 2 2000		
MAR 3 0 2000		
AUG 3 0 2000		
GAYLORD		PRINTED IN U.S.A.